2003

University of St. Francis Library

S0-BBT-287

VISIONS

Also by Marc Elihu Hofstadter

House of Peace

VISIONS

paintings by jackson pollock,
mark rothko, chang dai-chien, georgia o'keeffe
and california impressionists
seen through the optic of poetry

MARC ELIHU HOFSTADTER

Scarlet Tanager
BOOKS

UNIV. OF ST. FRANCIS
JOLIET, ILLINOIS

Copyright © 2001 by Marc Elihu Hofstadter.
All rights reserved.
Printed in the United States of America.

Cover painting: Mark Rothko, "Untitled, 1953 (Violet, Black,
Orange on Gray)," Gift of the Mark Rothko Foundation, Inc.,
Photograph © 2001 Board of Trustees, National Gallery of Art,
Washington, D.C.
Back cover photograph by G. Paul Bishop.
Design: DuFlon Design, Berkeley, CA.
Composition: Archetype Typography, Berkeley, CA.

Published by Scarlet Tanager Books
P.O. Box 20906
Oakland, CA 94620
www.scarlettanager.com

Library of Congress Cataloging-in-Publication Data

Hofstadter, Marc Elihu, 1945-
    Visions : paintings by Jackson Pollock, Mark Rothko,
Chang Dai-chien, Georgia O'Keeffe and California impressionists
seen through the optic of poetry / by Marc Elihu Hofstadter.
        p. cm.
    ISBN 0-9670224-5-2 (alk. paper)
1. Painting—Poetry. 2. Impressionism (Art)—Poetry. 3. California
in art—Poetry. I. Title.
    PS3608.O48 V57 2001
    811'.6—dc21
                                                    2001002990

811.6
H713

FOR DAVID

Contents

Acknowledgments

Alfred Levinson and David Mus set me on the path of poetry. Frédéric J. Grover taught me much of what I know about reading and understanding poems. Clive Matson reanimated my writing at a time when it was moribund. Gloria Suffin, Ralph Dranow and Leonard J. Cirino provided critical encouragement and evaluation. Lucille Lang Day believed in this book and made its publication possible. Kim Addonizio raised my writing to a higher level. Yves Bonnefoy provided an example of how poetry can transform one's life. Daniel Marlin, Mitchell Zeftel, David Schooley and Richard Woodruff furnished valuable feedback. My boss and friend Peter Straus lent me crucial support. My friends Arnold Suffin, Nicholas Follansbee, Firdosh Anklesaria, Don Sackheim, Gloria Grover, Willis Barnstone, Luis Garcia, Jannie Dresser, Gail Ford, Luther Freeman, Fannie Lee Lowe, Les Kong, Pamela Ong, William Hauser, Jane Falk, Richard and Peggy Kuhns, William Dickinson and August Bleed all contributed to this book with their sterling friendship. My partner and best friend David Zurlin taught me more than anyone else ever has about life and love.

Preface

I began writing "ekphrastic" poems—poems based on artworks in non-verbal media—in a "Crazy Child" workshop of Clive Matson's in January 1999. I had brought to the workshop Jeffrey Weiss's catalogue to the Rothko retrospective I saw in November 1998, a show that had made a big impression on me. I began to experiment with writing about these large, meditative, poetic paintings and the poems flowed—about thirty that day. I found the "translation" of my experience of a painting into words a very natural enterprise. When I look at a painting, one thing I do is talk to myself about it *sotto voce*: I say "This is doing this" and "He's suggesting this" and "This means that." I realize when I'm doing this that I'm a little *outside* the work, that I'm *interpreting* and not *living* it. So I don't let myself do it too much. I plunge back into the work, swirl around in it, let it take me over. But then—since as an observer I am not *in* the painting but separate from it—I detach a little again, become intellectual and restart interpreting. I believe works of art, even abstract paintings, express meaning, and the most common human method of experiencing meaning is through words. So why not try to convey the meaning of a non-verbal work in words? Of course, the effort is ultimately and inherently futile. Paintings, sculptures, pieces of music exist in their particular media because that's where they've been created. They solve specific problems in paint, stone, wood, sound that do not exist in any other media. But, as with the translation of literary works from one language into another, even though the project is hopeless people try all the time, and produce works of value.

Translating a painting into words is more adequately done with a poem than with a discursive statement. Since art is non-rational and intuitive, logical discourse can't describe it. But a poem, being a piece of language that's by its nature irrational, is better equipped than any other type of language to account for a painting's meaning. Poets have written poems about paintings at least since Jacopo Sadoleto created "On the Statue of Laocoon" in the sixteenth century. (John Hollander, *The Gazer's Spirit: Poems Speaking to Silent Works of Art,* University of Chicago Press, 1995, pages 97-98.) My first exposure to ekphrastic poetry was William Carlos Williams' wonderful "Pictures from Brueghel" in *Pictures from Brueghel and Other Poems,* New Directions, 1962. An exemplary ekphrastic work of our time from which I've learned a lot is Lynne Knight's *Snow Effects: Poems on "Impressionists in Winter,"* Small Poetry Press, Concord, California, 2000. All of these poems seek to do the impossible, and do it well. I hope my "visions" do justice to this strong and honorable tradition.

My "readings" of these paintings certainly do not claim to be definitive. There are many, indeed an infinity of ways to react to a work of art. My readings are highly subjective and personal. You'll note that, in each of these poems, I engage in the fiction that *I'm the painter* talking, so to speak, from inside the painting and having a privileged perspective on its meaning. In fact, of course, I have no such privileged knowledge. I do this in order to say what I think the painter "meant" by his or her painting—to immerse myself in the work so intimately that it's as though I *were* its creator. Don't we all, at heart, do this when we view a work of art? Leave our own existence behind to live vicariously in the mind of the work's creator? By speaking as though I were Jackson Pollock I'm merely formalizing this fiction. And trying to convey to you my particular experience of his works.

I didn't sit down and choose which artists I was going to write about in this book. They chose me. They represent the visual works that made the deepest impressions on me in 1998, 1999 and 2000. They're a diverse group: two New York Abstract Expressionists, a New York-New Mexico painter with disparate influences, a twentieth-century Chinese painter who lived for many years in the United States but is not well known here, and a group of amazing artists working in California in the first half of that century, also not widely known. If they hold together here, it's through the passion of my own particular style and vision. Vision is an amazing thing—each of us sees the world through our own unique eyes yet can share our visions through the human medium of language. In language, in some ways better than paint, stone or music, we can commune with one another.

A Note on the Paintings

I viewed all but one of the paintings described in this book at five marvelous exhibits: the 1998-99 Jackson Pollock retrospective at the Museum of Modern Art in New York City, the 1998 Mark Rothko retrospective, which I saw at the Whitney Museum in New York (it was organized by the National Gallery of Art in Washington, D.C.), the 1999 "Chang Dai-chien in California" show at San Francisco State University (co-sponsored by the National Museum of History of the Republic of China), the exhibit "All Things Bright & Beautiful: California Impressionist Paintings from the Irvine Museum," which I saw at the Oakland Museum in 1999, and the show "Georgia O'Keeffe: The Poetry of Things" organized by the Phillips Collection of Washington, D. C. in association with the Dallas Museum of Art, which I viewed at the Palace of the Legion of Honor in San Francisco in 2000. The only painting I haven't seen "live" is the very last one in my Rothko series, the remarkable "Untitled, 1970" reproduced in David Anfam's *catalogue raisonné, Mark Rothko: The Works on Canvas,* Yale University Press and the National Gallery, 1998, plate 834—Rothko's final work on canvas.

I've taken the titles of all the Rothko works on canvas from this Anfam volume. In cases in which I've written about more than one painting titled "Untitled" produced in a single year, I've added to this title the Anfam plate number, so that the reader who wants to look at the painting can know exactly which one it is. For Rothko works not on canvas, my titles come from the catalogue of the 1998 National Gallery of Art exhibit, edited by Jeffrey Weiss. Here, where more than one painting from a particular year bears the title "Untitled," I've furnished the Weiss plate number.

xiii

FIFTEEN PAINTINGS
BY JACKSON POLLOCK

Lucifer, 1947

The world's crazy with paint.
Dripping colors, for me, is living,
like a pilot with his jet
or Marilyn Monroe with her hips.
I swish and swagger with my stick and can
until the paint's alive and shaking
like an alligator thrashing its tail
in a teeming swamp.
I drip black, green, a little orange, a bit of red—
every color's in my grasp.
I exclude nothing.
I welcome squiggle, bump and streak.
I splash them out on the naked canvas
until it's live as a lake of fish,
as jazz, as me and my baby
making it all night.

Alchemy, 1947

I'd like to decipher this life of streaks, circles and blobs
but it's so dense I can't see,
so crowded I can't feel.
I can't interpret what things mean.
I can only set down in black, gray, white, red, orange, blue and
    yellow
what painting feels like
in a world of enigmas and turbulence.

Number 1A, 1948

White and black pigment leap from my stick
to splatter all over the canvas
like skaters careening around Rockefeller Center
or water-beetles skimming the surface of a pond.
Life's a mad dash into oblivion
so I rush around the painting
like a vehicle out of control,
throwing out arcs and slapping splashes,
letting my body follow the throbbing colors
on their loops around the vast, teeming canvas.

White Cockatoo: Number 24A, 1948

These birds are wacky
in their absurd jungle of leaves and cries.
Each bird's a fragment:
blue parrot peeks out,
red toucan sharpens its beak,
white cockatoo screams.
Feathers fly everywhere.
No human knows the secret of this jokey jungle.

Number 13A, 1948: Arabesque

Labyrinthine lines of Arab legend
fill my head with spirals and curlicues.
I swirl white, black and gray
against a background of Euphrates mud.
I make music, slow and sinuous
that leads a languid dance
around the elegant canvas.
Each step's the twirl of a delicate toe,
each curve the sweep of a brown calf
in love with dancing.

Summertime: Number 9A, 1948

Yes, the living's easy.
The sky's bright yellow over Central Park.
Kids shoot hoops on black asphalt
all over the city.
People laugh vermilion laughs.
Everything else is green.
Summer's happening again and forever.

Out of the Web: Number 7, 1949

Half-human shapes emerge from turbid waters
where ocean grasses sway back and forth.
Severed head.
Cracked fibula.
Torn sleeve.
I'd like to break through,
paint people sometimes.
Begin here,
with fragments?

Number 2, 1949

White, green, yellow, red
splatter on brown sky.
Stars, planets, comets, asteroids, meteors
race around
in endless overlappings.
Nebulae crash into supernovas.
Milky Ways stream across space.
The universe is electric!

Number 3, 1950

The city's a jungle—
snow, sun, ochre leaves, people, traffic
clogging every street and park
until the mind's dizzy
with the clot and swirl of things,
the full-to-the-brim weather.

Number 7, 1950

There's beauty in control:
broad strokes of gray
laced with streaks of white, black and yellow
against a beige background tinged with orange.
This design resembles
a Japanese calligrapher's graceful letters
or an autumn day full of contentment.

Number 32, 1950

Lines, blobs and squiggles are my alphabet of the absurd.
Little gnats flying intricate patterns
in icy air.
Curious characters leading
hectic urban lives.
Dancers in black pumps
tripping daintily
across the white dance floor.
My delicate calligraphy
of silence.

One: Number 31, 1950

No room to breathe
in this cacophony of snow,
soot, pigeons and people
they call the city.
Take a step and mud splashes.
Look out your window,
a man's died on the sidewalk.
Snowflakes bite your cheeks
as the wind whips around the corner of the mind
but my hand dares the cold,
spilling the city's lifeblood
all over the canvas.

Autumn Rhythm: Number 30, 1950

Dead leaves, snow and blacktop
sing a chilly autumn music.
The weather's elegant and loopy.
Cold air's alive.
Taxis, shoppers, squirrels race around
leaving tracks everywhere.
Things will die with winter
but I'll fix these movements
in absorbent paint
to preserve a piece of New York in autumn.

Number 1, 1952

Black-robed Japanese dancer
whirls through city streets—
headstands, pirouettes, cartwheels.
People join in,
squiggles of white, yellow, red, blue.
Secretaries throw office doors open.
Doormen dance the rumba on sidewalks.
Trees shake their limbs and shout.
Buildings cry Joy! Joy!

Blue Poles: Number 11, 1952

The world's in heat.
I can't breathe.
Is it day or night?
It's fireworks hour.
The swirl and fret of the mind
explodes into color.
The little world of self
becomes big as the fiery universe,
my soul's scream
splayed out on the canvas
held together by eight blue poles
swaying and whistling in the cosmic wind.

FIFTY PAINTINGS
BY MARK ROTHKO

Untitled, 1947
(Anfam, plate 359)

> Life's a busy child
> So many blue things to do
> Poke your finger in this red
> Stroke that white
> Are plants green?
> I like being a child

Untitled, 1948
(Anfam 370)

> I remember childhood lakes
> with sylvan trees, dreamy clouds
> and orange flowers
> I liked to swim
> There were fish
> But this is far away now
> as though behind a scrim

No. 19, 1949

I'm an artist trying to make a work
I've learned to draw well
so I put this white line here,
shade this yellow rectangle just so
and make the orange glow
But it's not quite right
It expresses my soul
but not all of it

No. 8 (Multiform), 1949

This is my first painting,
my first real painting
I've painted many before
but this time the red floats
above the bottom, just barely,
yet is solid
like my life,
for I'm established,
have a home and wife
yet am floating into myself
for the first time
Life is full of yellow, glowing light
I put it down
at the top
of my first painting

Untitled, 1949
(Weiss, plate 42)

I've got it down
I know how to create,
how to make colors glow,
composition suggest movement
and lines look just right
I'll put blue brushstrokes here
and red squiggles there
But it's not quite right
It's not from my heart

No. 3/No. 13 (Magenta, Black, Green on Orange), 1949

I'm starting to learn my themes:
death is black
I'll put it near the center
surrounded by magenta, white and green
I'll have them all float
on an orange background,
my favorite color
Life is poetic
like glowing rectangles

Untitled, 1949
(Anfam 425)

> *This* is my first painting
> All of it before was just practice
> I wasn't trying hard today,
> woke from a nap,
> put brush to canvas—
> yellow and orange, mauve and green—
> and a great black tomb in the center
> I discover who I am here
> I know death will always be part of me
> But death is part of nature—
> see how the green bleeds through the black

White Center (Yellow, Pink and Lavender on Rose), 1950

> Life's beyond words
> I burn with its yellows and roses
> I'm centered in white
> Death is a black line
> I'm a great pink shape
> that's so dazzling it blinds

No. 10, 1950

Sunshine, sky and clouds
are my faithful friends
all day today

No. 7, 1951

How little needs to be said
My yellow theme...
Orange fuels it
At the top, a small purple cloud
merges into the sun

No. 2/No. 7/No. 20, 1951

The sun burns intensely
through hazy sky on snow
The green pond's covered with ice
My eyes delight in this
Japanese print of a world

No. 25 (Red, Gray, White on Yellow), 1951

Illness clouds everything
You almost think the sun has disappeared
behind fog
Death is present—
you could draw a black line and say,
this is it
Your body burns
like a funeral pyre
I draw a white line through the black and wait

No. 18, 1951

Sometimes I'm not sure
whether white reminds me of the chill of death
or the glow of God
It shines through a slit in the red,
disappears,
then suddenly pours down,
covering everything
I don't know whether to flee
or laugh

Untitled (Blue, Green and Brown), 1952

I've always been fearful
but here I am in mid-ocean
with friends—
green, brown and blue creatures
We float half-asleep,
glowing

No. 10, 1952

I play like a child,
reducing my big themes
to a manageable design,
smudging red into yellow,
blue into green
as though there were no urgency to things

Untitled (Violet, Black, Orange on Gray), 1953

Maybe I talk too much about death
but here it looms
Is there something behind it,
seeping through—
orange?
The violet sky
stretches almost to the horizon

White, Orange and Yellow, 1953

There are two of us
We vibrate together
One is white, the other yellow
Our fuzzy borders almost touch
We float,
two friends happy at being near one another

No. 61 (Rust and Blue)(Brown, Blue, Brown on Blue), 1953

We live between twin mysteries—
is sky's blue behind
or ahead?
An enigma hovers,
a muddle floats—
we're in between

Untitled (Purple, White and Red), 1953

Here's shark purple,
here blood red
Between them I outline,
in an empty shape,
all the possibilities I hope
exist free of shark or blood

No. 1 (Royal Red and Blue)(Untitled), 1954

Sunlight is so hot
it almost burns
Deep sky floats beneath

Untitled (Blue, Yellow, Green on Red), 1954

The sun shines
everywhere today,
dwarfing green nature
and death's little black cloud

Yellow and Blue (Yellow, Blue on Orange), 1955

I like Manhattan—
the sun glazes a million windows,
skyscrapers are busy,
the sky over the Palisades's a deep blue
On days like this
the city's one great cathedral

No. 46 (Black, Ochre, Red Over Red), 1957

Death won't leave me
Its black mixes with red
to form mud, blood

Black Over Reds (Black on Red), 1957

Sometimes death makes me blaze
like the hottest fire

No. 13 (White, Red on Yellow), 1958

Clouds are molded shapes today,
textured and full
The sun is a red, naked eye,
unwavering
The medium that allows both to exist,
light, surrounds them

No. 10, 1958

Death stings—
I'm sick
Anger glowers and roils in me
like red clouds
The sky's black as night

UNIV. OF ST. FRANCIS
JOLIET, ILLINOIS

Lavender and Mulberry, 1959

Blue and white jump in me
like happy amoebas merging
into one peaceful lavender square

Untitled, 1959
(Weiss 81)

Sometimes life's joys are small—
a little orange square,
a yellow one,
a magenta line in between

No. 7, 1960

Time passes—
I'm growing old
I don't feel comfortable
with this awkward body,
this fatigue
Yet clouds are still white

No. 14, 1960

Lurid sunset and dark blue sky
expand in flying mist
until I can't see anything
but the vibration of colors
and feel like screaming

No. 2/No. 101, 1961

I don't find death very pleasant
nor do I like the way
I'm sucked down into green and blue depths
as the sun burns up above

No. 1 (White and Red), 1962

Death...

sunset...

clouds...

Blue and Gray, 1962

A gray cloud vibrates
The ocean gapes deep and dark
It's raining
and will never stop

No. 3 (Bright Blue, Brown, Dark Blue on Wine), 1962

Nothing stirs
Even light doesn't vibrate any more
The sky's dead

No. 2 (Untitled), 1963

This is it
I can't breathe
There's hardly any light
Only, near the sky,
a strange orange glow

Untitled, 1963
(Anfam 743)

There are many deaths
They stretch out like great coffins
across the vast sky
And there's a cloud
that looks just like them

Untitled (White, Blacks, Grays on Maroon), 1963

Static blocks of black
press out all the world's air
One cloud tries to keep the faith

Untitled, 1964
(Weiss 97)

Nature's green almost crowds me out
It's beautiful
but I'm not part of it any more,
I'm drab and dull

No. 8, 1964
(Weiss 100)

It's as though I've already died
Nothing's left
except a faint purple in the air

Untitled, 1968
(Anfam 812)

Death conquers all
yet there's movement
in the dark sea below it

Untitled, 1968
(Weiss 105)

>Rain and dark skies
>blur under my brushstrokes
>into sad, playful shapes

Untitled, 1968
(Weiss 106)

>I'm grateful for small things
>A fuzzy blue-green square likes me
>An intense red rectangle grins

Untitled, 1969
(Weiss 107)

> The world, small and brown,
> floats in an immensity of blue

Untitled, 1969
(Weiss 108)

> It's hard to say
> anything
> I'd like to dazzle you
> with luminous red and magenta shapes,
> sunlight and death,
> oaks, the sea and human faces
> All that is not for me
> The world is black,
> but for a moment I'll play
> with shades of gray and lilac
> I make them shine with a light
> I no longer see
> except here

Untitled, 1969
(Weiss 109)

> What's this color?
> I've never seen it before
> I'm in an unexplored world

Untitled, 1969
(Weiss 110)

> I remember life's delights
> though they're gone from me now
> I remember red, I remember blue

Untitled, 1969
(Weiss 111)

> I brush slate blue paint,
> carmine, sky blue
> They're on the surface only,
> for that's all that can be seen
> except the background
> reality, white,
> which is unknown to us

Untitled (Black on Gray), 1969-70
(Anfam 830)

> I divide things simply now—
> lunar surface,
> black sky
> How empty space is

Untitled (Black on Gray), 1969
(Anfam 825)

> Life, death...
> White, black...
> I set them down
> for the last time

Untitled, 1970
(Anfam 834)

> Afterword:
> afterimage of the sun
> that blinds,
> red you see
> after you've seen everything
> Fire, blood, the deepest eye
> Done

TWENTY PAINTINGS
BY CALIFORNIA IMPRESSIONISTS

Alfred Mitchell's "Sunset Glow, California"

Distant mountains glow like ebbing coals.
The valley below's cool as a swallow's wing.
Eucalyptus raise clattering leaves to the breeze.
Bushes and rocks litter the hills near me.
I sit and gaze.
Paradise.

Theodore Wores' "A Saratoga Road"

I stroll on this road
through a pear orchard.
Blossoms are little white flags.
A few are red.
The hills beyond are purple with pine
and roll like a woman's breasts and hips.
Beneath my feet
fresh dirt,
wet grass.
I pass through this morning
of petals and dew.

Alfred Mitchell's "In Morning Light"

Sun's beginning to warm the air.
Sand's still cool and wet between my toes.
A fresh breeze wets my face.
Cliffs tower over me.
I may swim later
or take one of these dinghies out.
For now I just look at this morning light,
this light.

Bruce Nelson's "The Summer Sea"

The sea, calm and sapphire blue,
rocks gently back and forth.
Sun relaxes my body.
Cliffs are bright beige,
fields green with artichokes and Brussels sprouts.
I'll walk all day today in the heat
feeling cool grass between my toes.

William Wendt's "I Lifted Mine Eyes Unto the Hills"

I lifted mine eyes unto the hills,
green and blue in sun and shade,
and as they rose high into the cloud-swirled sky
I soared up to fly with God.

William Ritschel's "Purple Tide"

The sea's purple—
with algae they say
but I think it's a god
who raises these bulging billows,
shatters waves against mussel-crowded rocks,
splashes drops on my face.
This god is mine,
he roils and rages in me,
we stir the sea to madness
before crashing, exhausted,
against the cliffs.

Arthur Hill Gilbert's "Land of Gray Dunes, Monterey"

The sky glowers
as I walk among dunes
feeling cold wind,
dreading I know not what,
finding a few yellow wildflowers
poking out of wet sand.

Benjamin Brown's "The Joyous Garden"

Red and white flowers in the garden:
I think of my love
and the burgeoning day
and afternoons by the sea
and my child's garden of pansies and radishes
and my mother's face
and sniffing sweet air
and being born.

Alson S. Clark's "The Weekend, Mission Beach"

Dad pitches the tent.
Mom makes sandwiches.
We play.
No one else here.
Sand, stones, little plants.
No noise except the wind
and the waves' hiss.
The sky's bigger
than any dream I've ever had.

Paul Dougherty's "The Twisted Ledge"

I stand on a twisted ledge
afraid yet almost wanting to fall into the sea,
deep blue and comforting.
The rocks are golden brown friends.
Shall I clamber down?

Guy Rose's "Incoming Tide"

Tide's coming in.
Scary.
Water froths white and icy.
Rocks reflect a surreal light.
I stand still, petrified.

Theodore Wores' "A Hillside in Saratoga"

Bright sun casts shadows of plum trees
down the steep slope where I stand
gazing at pink blossoms and blue spring sky,
trying to keep my balance.

Marion Kavanagh Wachtel's "Landscape with Oak Trees"

Live oaks cling to hillsides
like precious memories of childhood.
Below, the valley,
gray and final.

William F. Jackson's "Radiant Valley"

I walk in meadows of orange poppies,
blue lupine and lush grass.
Full trees rise on either side.
Far away a town,
beyond it purple, then white mountains.
Land of my dreams.

Guy Rose's "Mist Over Point Lobos"

High up, Monterey pines cling to cliffs.
Mists shift and flow.
Boulders jut up.
Below, the sea
heaves, splashes and roars
like a monster.

Charles Reiffel's "Summer"

Golden hills strewn
with eucalyptus trunks and stripped bark.
Some trees still green.
I walk among boulders,
my body drenched in light.

Guy Rose's "Laguna Eucalyptus"

My dead friend John,
these eucalyptus have that pungent scent you loved
in their gray-green, messy hairdos.
I miss you.

William Wendt's "There Is No Solitude, Even in Nature"

Hills are full of jagged rocks.
Grasses are sparse, almost brown.
In the distance, purple mountains.
Above them, the moon
in a blue, Van Gogh twilight sky.
I stand on a hill,
the sun still burning behind me
throwing shadows on the rocks below.
We are not alone.

Edgar Payne's "The Sierra Divide"

I've come this far
but these mountains,
high, sharp, gray,
block my way.
I'll hike down to the lake,
stay as long as I can.

William Wendt's "The Silent Summer Sea"

The sea's quiet today, absolutely still.
It stretches out forever.
I stand here in sunlight
that also seems eternal.

TEN PAINTINGS
BY CHANG DAI-CHIEN

Spring Clouds, 1965

In me two streams converge:
the colorful poetry of Ryder, Dove, Nolde
and the precise delicacy
of Ma Lin, Wu Chen, Shen Chou.
I make washes of blue, green and white
that are fresh clouds floating,
lyrical as a child's dream,
impermanent as mist.

Temple in the Mountains, 1966

Temple perched on crag deep in secret forest.
For me Eastern wisdom meets Western freedom
in how splashed blue and green support
the careful lineation of architecture.
Wordsworth greets Po Chü-i.

Summer on California Mountain, 1967

This gold mountain, my California dream.
Sun's rays fan from its summit
like a Giotto halo.
Sky and clouds are angels' vestments.
Green torrents cascade down ravines.
Evil's black fingers clutch up from below.
I'm of China and see darkness
as part of the brightest sun,
yin in yang, the Tao in everything.
Here the West of sunshine meets
the delicate poetry of my childhood,
splashed black
blends with dazzling gold.

Finger Painting: Splashed Ink on Fiberglass, 1967

A thousand stories in these splashes:
Chinese calligraphy or Pollock drips?
I state ideas in careful splats,
lose myself in wide arcs.
I found ancient wisdom in New York,
adventure in Shanghai.

Red Hills Overshadowed by Snow, 1967

These Yunan hills could be the Rockies
the way snow rests on rugged peaks.
Red, white, green and blue mix,
calligrapher's ink becomes painter's pigment,
paint becomes poetry,
the landscapes of my country fuse
with the red hills of Utah.

Clouded Village, 1967

I've lived in this village a thousand years.
Set in among dense trees, my dwellings' delicate roofs
have not changed. Yet art makes things new—
my washes of blue, green, black and brown
freshen up the town, lend it modern raiments.
I'm in love with Motherwell and Wen Cheng-ming
and find perfection in the union of opposites.

Landscape, 1967

Carmel's transformed by my brush
into an ancient land governed by spirits.
Its mansions are flat-roofed temples,
its craggy coastline, grotesque gods.
My mind's suspended between two continents,
feeding on each,
drawing sustenance from their interpenetration.

Autumn Mountains in Twilight, 1967

Mountains here
and in China
glow equally at sunset.
The end of things
brings white and blue clouds
to float peacefully through a valley.
They form, dissolve and re-form.
Paint sifts and blurs like light.

Manchurian Mountains, 1969

My composition's precise yet my brushwork's bold.
Fog pushes its fingers over the hills of Manchuria
and California. I'm two people—
ancient truth and newfound beauty,
sliding fog and rigid pines,
movement and form.

Panorama of Mount Lu, 1983

I draw in black and brown ink
a panorama of crags, trees, dwellings, waterfall.
This is China, vast, unchanging.
But where the waterfall strikes earth
a great mist of blue and green paint churns up.
In California I knew life as vibrant color,
so here's my final wish:
glowing mist and eternal land one forever.

FIFTEEN PAINTINGS
BY GEORGIA O'KEEFFE

Petunia II, 1924

> Two huge mauve blossoms float
> above the blue-green earth
> like sublime spaceships, divine sky-monsters.
> Awesome beauty, I am a painter
> who follows your orbits,
> submits to your power!

Leaf Motif #2, 1924

> Leaf whorls
> make bone swirls
> make human ears
> make ligatures of delight.

Morning Glory with Black, No. 3, 1926

A white hole is this flower
that sucks in bees, people, anything.
It's vastly indifferent,
faulted only by the black at its side.

Oriental Poppies, 1928

Two flowers crowd each other.
Orange fire thrusts and swirls.
Intense isn't intense enough.
All that counts is the desire to live.
Black pistils are the core
of this unending turbulence.

Brown and Tan Leaves, 1928

One large tan
and two small brown leaves
with skinlike texture
and fleshlike curves
pose next to each other,
sentient as humans.

The Lawrence Tree, 1929

I have a brown soul.
My branches reach like tentacles
into the starry sky.
My dark hair billows like clouds.
I blossom upward
into the infinite, my home.

From a Shell, 1930

Inside a shell
light pours down from its firmament
like forked lightning.
The sky's white
as the Day of Judgment.
The earth
isn't important any more,
so porous is it with light.

Dark and Lavender Leaf, 1931

A small lavender leaf
cradled by a large, velvet, dark one
like...son by mother?
lover by lover?
sentient being by sentient being?
Words can't convey the way
this art's design fixes
so equivocal an embrace.

Summer Days, 1936

Summer flowers in the sky,
death's head
over ancient peaks.

Pelvis with Pedernal, 1943

There's consciousness
in pelvic bones that fly
like eagles or spaceships
over spiritual mountains.

Pelvis with Blue (Pelvis I), 1944

I look through perfect white death
into infinity blue as a robin's egg.

Pelvis Series, Red with Yellow, 1945

This red and yellow egg,
this vulva,
this pelvic bone
blazes, still pulsing
from the Big Bang.

In the Patio #1, 1946

This window
flip-flops in the vision
into a geometric shape
as dazzling light
pours onto the adobe wall.

It Was Yellow and Pink II, 1959

Pink river branches out
across yellow terrain
like blood vessels
or leaves' ribbing
or my dreams striding into the future.

Winter Road I, 1963

The path in snow
follows the ink
of my final curve.

Index

No. 8, 1964 *(Weiss 100)*, *32*
No. 8 (Multiform), 1949, *14*
No. 10, 1950, *17*
No. 10, 1952, *20*
No. 10, 1958, *25*
No. 13 (White, Red on Yellow), 1958, *25*
No. 14, 1960, *27*
No. 18, 1951, *19*
No. 19, 1949, *14*
No. 25 (Red, Gray, White on Yellow), 1951, *18*
No. 46 (Black, Ochre, Red Over Red), 1957, *24*
No. 61 (Rust and Blue)(Brown, Blue, Brown on Blue), 1953, *21*
Untitled, 1947 *(Anfam 359)*, *13*
Untitled, 1948 *(Anfam 370)*, *13*
Untitled, 1949 *(Weiss 42)*, *15*
Untitled, 1949 *(Anfam 425)*, *16*
Untitled, 1959 *(Weiss 81)*, *26*
Untitled, 1963 *(Anfam 743)*, *30*
Untitled, 1964 *(Weiss 97)*, *31*
Untitled, 1968 *(Anfam 812)*, *32*
Untitled, 1968 *(Weiss 105)*, *33*
Untitled, 1968 *(Weiss 106)*, *33*
Untitled, 1969 *(Weiss 107)*, *34*
Untitled, 1969 *(Weiss 108)*, *34*
Untitled, 1969 *(Weiss 109)*, *35*
Untitled, 1969 *(Weiss 110)*, *35*
Untitled, 1969 *(Weiss 111)*, *36*
Untitled, 1970 *(Anfam 834)*, *37*
Untitled (Black on Gray), 1969 *(Anfam 825)*, *37*
Untitled (Black on Gray), 1969-70 *(Anfam 830)*, *36*
Untitled (Blue, Green and Brown), 1952, *19*
Untitled (Blue, Yellow, Green on Red), 1954, *23*
Untitled (Purple, White and Red), 1953, *22*
Untitled (Violet, Black, Orange on Gray), 1953, *20*
Untitled (White, Blacks, Grays on Maroon), 1963, *31*
White Center (Yellow, Pink and Lavender on Rose), 1950, *16*
White, Orange and Yellow, 1953, *21*
Yellow and Blue (Yellow, Blue on Orange), 1955, *23*

The Author

Marc Elihu Hofstadter was born in New York City in 1945 and grew up in the suburb of Larchmont, New York, and in Manhattan. He graduated from Horace Mann High School in 1963, earned a Bachelor of Arts degree from Swarthmore College in 1967 (majoring in French literature) and obtained a Master's degree in Literature in 1969 and a Ph.D. in the same field in 1975 from the University of California at Santa Cruz, writing his dissertation on the late poetry and the poetics of William Carlos Williams. He taught numerous classes at U.C. Santa Cruz, American literature and English language at the Université d'Orléans in France in 1977-78 and American literature at Tel Aviv University in 1978-79. In 1980 he received a Master's degree in Library and Information Studies from the University of California at Berkeley and since that time has worked as a librarian, including the past eighteen years as the Librarian of the San Francisco Municipal Railway, the City of San Francisco's transit agency. He is the author of a previous poetry collection, *House of Peace* (Mother's Hen, 1999), and has published poetry in *Talisman, Exquisite Corpse, The Hawai'i Review, Confrontation, Pearl, The Carquinez Review, Poetalk* and *Berkeley Works,* translations of Yves Bonnefoy's poetry in *Boundary 2* and *The Malahat Review,* essays in *The Redwood Coast Review,* and literary critical articles in *Twentieth Century Literature, The Romanic Review* and *Romance Notes.* He and his partner David Zurlin, an artist, have lived in the East Bay since they met in 1990.

Also from Scarlet Tanager Books:

Wild One by Lucille Lang Day
    poetry, 100 pages, $12.95

The "Fallen Western Star" Wars: A Debate About Literary California, edited by Jack Foley
    essays, 86 pages, $14.00

Catching the Bullet & Other Stories by Daniel Hawkes
    fiction, 64 pages, $12.95

red clay is talking by Naomi Ruth Lowinsky
    poetry, 142 pages, $14.95

Everything Irish by Judy Wells
    poetry, 112 pages, $12.95